TAKE ME TO THE RIVER

+

Rev. June Ferguson

Trilogy Christian Publishers

A Wholly Owned Subsidiary of Trinity Broadcasting Network

2442 Michelle Drive

Tustin, CA 92780

Copyright © 2023 by Rev. June Ferguson

Scripture quotations marked NKJV are taken from the New King James Version®. Copyright © 1982 by Thomas Nelson. Used by permission. All rights reserved.

All rights reserved, including the right to reproduce this book or portions thereof in any form whatsoever.

For information, address Trilogy Christian Publishing

Rights Department, 2442 Michelle Drive, Tustin, Ca 92780.

Trilogy Christian Publishing/ TBN and colophon are trademarks of Trinity Broadcasting Network.

For information about special discounts for bulk purchases, please contact Trilogy Christian Publishing.

Trilogy Disclaimer: The views and content expressed in this book are those of the author and may not necessarily reflect the views and doctrine of Trilogy Christian Publishing or the Trinity Broadcasting Network.

10 9 8 7 6 5 4 3 2 1

Library of Congress Cataloging-in-Publication Data is available.

ISBN 979-9-89041-605-6

ISBN (ebook) 979-9-89041-606-3

FOREWORD

The title of this book results from a childhood memory, when the local pastors, on certain Sundays after their church service, would invite their entire congregation to meet at a nearby river, to perform *immersion* baptisms.

Once there, the pastor would wade out a short distance into the water, until he was standing waist deep in the water, then, turning to face those standing on the bank of the river, he would invite those desiring to be baptized to stand in a line. One by one, each took their turn walking down into the river, to stand in front of the pastor.

The pastor would then place his hand on top of their head, say a short prayer over them, and then he would lean them backwards and dunk them under the water for a brief moment. Afterwards, he would pull them back up, thereby baptizing them.

*immersion: fully submerging a person's body in water (e.g, in a river)

My thoughts for today...

Take me to the river-
wash me clean!
Giving me new hopes-
and new dreams!

Give it all to God, trusting that He can handle it,
For God's hands are a lot bigger than yours or mine!

DEDICATION

This book is dedicated to everyone in the universe,
For we are *all* children of God!

This book, *Take Me to the River*, answers the question of why we baptize. The act of baptism is a symbolic gesture that *validates* our responsibility to believe in God's love and His absolute power. The act of baptism is our recognition of our decision to seek the will of God, *manifesting* agreement with *reverence*.

*validates: demonstrate or support the truth or value of

*manifesting: display or show (a quality or feeling) by one's acts or appearance; demonstrate

*reverence: deep respect for someone or something

"Then Jesus called a little child to Him, set him in the midst of them, and said, "Assuredly, I say to you, unless you are *converted* and become as little children, you will by no means enter the kingdom of heaven.'"

Matthew 18:2-3 (NKJV)

*converted: to bring over from one belief, view, or party to another

---

My thoughts for today...

Jesus died as a ramson to save many; when He spoke about being "converted," He was telling us that we will need to believe like a small child and accept Jesus Christ into our hearts, believing that He is the Son of God, in order to receive the gift of eternal life. This gift has already been paid for in full, and it's the gift that keeps on giving!

TABLE OF CONTENTS

PROLOGUE 11
FAST MOVING TRAIN 13
PREFACE 17
GOD IS REAL 21
LOVE EACH OTHER 23
THE TRUE NATURE OF GOD 25
ALL THE PEOPLE OF THE UNIVERSE ARE CHILDREN OF GOD 31
LOVE ABOVE ALL ELSE 33
JESUS THE CORNERSTONE 35
MERCY, NOT SACRIFICE 37
REJOICE 39
THE GOOD SHEPHERD 41
JESUS DOES NOT JUDGE 43
JESUS WAS A GOD-SEND 45
FREE INDEED 47
THE DEVIL IS A LIAR 49
BORN OF GOD 51
FULFILLMENT OF GOD'S WILL 53
THE WAY, THE TRUTH, AND THE LIFE 55
THE PROMISED ONE 57
HATED BY THE WORLD 59
CONFIDENCE IN PRAYER 61
KNOWING THE TRUE, REJECTING THE FALSE 63
OBEDIENCE BY FAITH 65
THE GREAT AND AWESOME DAY OF THE LORD 67
JESUS PRAYING IN THE GARDEN 71
ANOINTING OF JESUS' FEET 73
CAIAPHAS PROPHESIED CONCERNING JESUS 75
JESUS RAISED LAZARUS FROM THE DEAD 77
PLOT TO KILL LAZARUS 79
JESUS RODE A LOWLY DONKEY INTO JERUSALEM 81
DO NOT WEEP FOR ME 83
PARADISE 85
CAUGHT UP INTO PARADISE 87
GUARDIAN ANGELS 91
JESUS FULFILLED HIS DESTINY 95
BLESSED BY BELIEVING 97
PROMISE OF THE FATHER 99
WHEN JESUS RETURNS 103
JESUS EXALTED ABOVE THE ANGELS 105
HOPE DOES NOT DISAPPOINT 107
SWEET-SMELLING AROMA 109
MY CUP RUNNETH OVER 111

FEARLESS	113
MY LORD, MY SHEPHERD	115
KNOWING GOD	117
THE GOOD NEWS	119
THE KINGDOM BELONGS TO THE LORD	121
TEMPTATION	123
FOLLOW ME	125
IT IS FINISHED	127
HOPE IN THE LORD	129
SET FREE	131
GOD CAN DO THE IMPOSSIBLE	133
THE ALPHA AND OMEGA	135
JESUS IS BOTH LORD AND CHRIST	137
GOD IS LONG-SUFFERING	139
JESUS LAY DOWN HIS LIFE	141
MEDITATION	143
JOHN THE BAPTIST PREPARES THE WORLD	145
FISHER OF MEN	147
WHERE ARE YOU, LORD?	149
GOD WILL PROVIDE	151
BROKEN SPIRIT	153
DON'T LOSE HEART	155
SPIRITUAL GIFTS	157
BLESSED WHEN WE TRUST GOD	159
NO CLOCKS IN HEAVEN	161
GOSSIP	163
NOTHING TOO HARD FOR GOD	165
IF TWO AGREE	167
VALUE OF A FRIEND	169
ALL THINGS MADE NEW	171
OUR FATHER	173
IN GOD WE TRUST	175
JESUS ASCENDS TO HEAVEN	177
SAVING THE WORLD	179
DO NOT THROW STONES	181
THE SON OF GOD	183
BE PREPARED	185
GOOD AND EVIL	189
REMEMBER ME	193
OUR TIMES ARE IN GOD'S HANDS	195
I AM WITH YOU ALWAYS	197
LOVE IS THE MAIN INGREDIENT	199
KEEP MOVING FORWARD	201
LOSS OF A LOVED ONE	203
TRUST IN GOD	205
GIFT OF THE HOLY SPIRIT	209
AFTERWORD	213

PROLOGUE

If you are waiting until you get it right--
And are leading the perfect life or lifestyle--
Before accepting Jesus into your heart and your life--
You never will.
For who is perfect?
And who is without sin?
No one!
And let me assure you that you will NEVER be perfect!
For even after we accept Jesus into our hearts--
And even after we are baptized--
We will still sin.
For we are human.
But the Bible tells us there is sin not leading to death--
And there is sin leading to death.
And the sin leading to death is to NOT accept Jesus Christ.
For Jesus is the Way.
Jesus is the ONLY way--
To gain entry into heaven and to have eternal life.
Amen.

FAST MOVING TRAIN

There is a fast-moving train traveling throughout the Universe,

tooting its horn and picking up speed.

The train's conductor is calling out your name,

and inviting you to come aboard.

The Conductor's name is Jesus Christ

and the boarding tickets He hands out read "Heaven-bound",

and they are free!

So, hop aboard, all;

because you don't want to miss *this* train

as its final destination is Paradise!

The children's story of Pinocchio is a good scenario of God and His creation. For God is our Creator and He designed each one of us as an original. Furthermore, He made us in His own image and lovingly made us His children. In fact, God loves us so much that He did not want us to be just puppets, so He gave to each of us—our own "free will!"

The disciples and apostles in the Holy Bible were in reality
following their own spiritual journey.
When things did not fit into their new way of thinking,
They would discard the old and put on the new—
passionately sharing this in their writings.
While staying in their own lane,
They ran their race until they reached the finish line.
Where most of them gave their lives
rather than relinquish their newfound beliefs.

PREFACE

This book is written using the Holy Bible as its primary reference, the teaching of Jesus, God, and love. As my spiritual journey continued, I became deeply aware of the importance of including love with anything dealing with God because we are taught that GOD *IS* LOVE.

That being said, my emphasis is on the Bible because I believe these writings are actually from God to all of us and the writers were men that God chose, inspired, and equipped to share God's love with us.

I firmly believe that God IS love; thus, anything dealing with God *must* include and embody love. In like manner, anything that does not include love is *not* of God.

This book is not intended as an educational interpretation of the Bible. I am not an expert or a highly educated Bible scholar. I am simply and humbly writing about my own spiritual journey. I wish to share part of that journey, for I consider it my treasure and my calling.

My hope is that this book, *Take Me to the River*, will encourage and inspire each of you to have your own personal relationship with God.

My desire is that you will open your Bible, read it with fresh eyes, the way I did, forgetting all that you have ever heard or read, and re-read it with a childlike wonder. The wonder of realizing that God IS Love, that each and every person in the universe is His beloved child, and that He loves us unconditionally. I pray that this realization will set you free, for then you will know the truth: that we are more precious to our Heavenly Father than we could ever imagine and that Jesus Christ died for us so that we might have life, and life more abundantly.

God desires that we have an abundant life here on earth, not just in the hereafter. It all begins with us remembering that He is with us always.

Our Heavenly Father is many wonderful things:

He is powerful, miraculous, and merciful but most of all—God is love!

GOD IS REAL

First of all, God *IS*. There *is* a God. God may be called by many names, but the God that created us as individual, eternal spirits is the same no matter what name is used. God is *real* and we are His children.

God is the Creator of everything and everyone, no matter our geography, language, or the color of our skin. All the people of the universe are God's children and as any parent feels when rejected by a child, when we turn away from God, it saddens His loving heart.

God's very nature is LOVE and when He created us, the ability to love was put inside each one of us as a part of our DNA. God also gave us a free will, so it is our choice to love God and to love others, or to not love at all. Love is always at the center of our nature, but we may choose to ignore that love or choose to express it in life. Truly, love is a choice that we make, every second of the day.

However, if we choose not to love God, we are choosing to be alienated; but that alienation comes from us and not from God. Our Heavenly Father has not and will never stop loving us. The proof of God's love was demonstrated in the actions of Jesus Christ when He suffered and died on the cross, as a ramson to save many.

Jesus loves us, whether it be yellow, white, black, red, or brown, for we were all made by God's design, which makes us all precious in His sight.

Today is the first day of the rest of our lives,
so, let's enjoy it by living in the moment!

LOVE EACH OTHER

"Jesus said unto him, 'You shall love the Lord your God with all your heart, with all your soul, and with all your mind.' This is the first and great commandment.

And the second is like it; 'You shall love your neighbor as yourself.' On these two commandments hang all the Law and the Prophets."
Matthew 22:37-40 (NKJV)

"Therefore, whatever you want men to do to you do also to them, for this is the Law and the Prophets."
Matthew 7:12 (NKJV)

My thoughts for today…

THE TEN COMMANDMENTS

Did you know that the Ten Commandments were based upon the concept of love, with the emphasis on showing love not only to God, but to each other?

For example, if you bear false witness, you are hurting someone by lying concerning them.

If you steal from someone, you are hurting them by taking what they have.

If you commit adultery with someone, you are hurting that person's husband or wife.

By now, you get the idea and you can finish these on your own.

COUNT YOUR BLESSINGS

Don't know where to start?

Did you know that every heartbeat is a blessing from God?

Your heart is about the size of your fist and is protected by your ribs and breastbone (sternum), and beats about 100,000 times a day,

This shows how richly blessed you are every single day of your life!

THE TRUE NATURE OF GOD

We have all questioned what God is really like, and I believe the answer can best be found in the Parable of the Prodigal Son, as told by Jesus. This parable, on the surface, appears to be a noteworthy story of a father showing forgiveness to his son. But it is a great deal more, because Jesus was actually describing the true nature of our Heavenly Father.

The Prodigal Son parable portrays a father having two sons, both whom he loved dearly. The father planned to leave each son an inheritance one day. However, while the elder son was content to wait, the second son was not; for the second son wanted his inheritance here and now. The son's goal to obtain his inheritance early stemmed from a desire to leave home and live in the city, which had more to offer a young man. The father knew that doing this was not in the best interest of his son, so he refused the son's request.

The son would not take no for an answer and persisted in asking for his share of the inheritance. Finally, the father relented and handed him his share of the inheritance. A short time later, the father watched sadly as his son took the money and walked away from his father and family.

Upon the son's arrival in the city, he sought out the nightlife, with all its activities, and began enjoying a carefree and uninhibited lifestyle. The son shared his newfound wealth with his new formed friends and enjoyed the attention of many women. He was having the time of his life and living a lifestyle where there was a party every day.

However, after a short time, the money ran out—he had spent every single penny. He was dismayed to discover that he had no money left. Dumbfounded, he turned to his friends for help, but to his surprise, they all simply walked away. All his new friends were no longer interested in being his friend because he had nothing left, and no money, to offer them.

The son decided to seek a job in order to purchase food but this turned out to be harder than he expected. The only work he found that he was skilled to do was feeding pigs. During that time and culture many years ago, pigs were considered the lowest form of animal. The son labored long hours while feeling humiliated at doing such a lowly job. Plus, the pangs of hunger were gnawing at his stomach.

The son watched the pigs scrambling and devouring the scraps of food he fed them and felt envy that they had food while he had nothing to eat. Eventually, his hunger pains could no longer be ignored and he even contemplated eating the food, called slop, fed to the pigs.

It was this thought, to eat the pig's slop, that brought him to his senses.

He decided to go to his father and beg for work as a servant, for he remembered how well his father treated all his servants.

Shortly thereafter, the son left the city and headed back home.

While he walked toward his boyhood home, he rehearsed what he was going to say to his father once he arrived back home. Although feeling unworthy, the crestfallen son desperately hoped his father would take him on as a servant.

The son was astonished when his father, who had been watching daily, hoping for his son's safe return, saw him from afar and ran to greet him with tears of joy.

Even before the son could say a word, his father embraced him, overjoyed to have his son safely back home. The father hurried his servants to fetch the best robe and slippers and he put them on his son, atop the smell of pigs and grime. The son was speechless, overcome with emotion, upon seeing the love in his father's eyes and his complete lack of judgement. Ultimately, the son had grown even more precious in his father's eyes at the thought of losing him forever.

Jesus, in telling this story, was teaching us that God is *our* Father and we are His beloved children. Moreover, the parable teaches us that our Heavenly Father's love, just like the son's father's, is unconditional.

For that very reason, we don't need to try to earn God's love – we simply need to realize that *WE ARE LOVED!*

My thoughts for today…

The world may look at you as being insignificant, but God sees you as the apple of His eye!

ALL THE PEOPLE OF THE UNIVERSE ARE CHILDREN OF GOD

"For you are all sons of God through faith in Christ Jesus.

For as many of you as were baptized into Christ have put on Christ.

There is neither Jew nor Greek,

There is neither slave or free,

There is neither male nor female;

For you are all one in Christ Jesus.

And if you are Christ's,

Then you are Abraham's seed,

And heirs according to the promise."

Galatians 3:26-29 (NKJV)

My thoughts for today...

Everyone in the universe is a child of God
Which makes each of us--

brothers and sisters!

Stop and think back,
When was the last time
That you were truly still
And spent time with your Heavenly Father?

LOVE ABOVE ALL ELSE

"Above all things have fervent love for each other, for love will cover a multitude of sins."

Peter 4:7-8 (NKJV)

"Though I speak with the tongues of men and of angels, but have not love, I have become sounding brass or a clanging cymbal. And though I have the gift of prophecy and understand all mysteries an all knowledge, and though I have all faith, so that I can move mountains, but have not love, I am nothing. And though I bestow all my goods to feed the poor, and though I give my body to be burned, but have not love, it profits me nothing. Love suffers long and is kind; Love does not envy; Love does not parade itself, is not puffed up; Does not behave rudely, does not see its own, is not provoked, thinks no evil, does not rejoice in iniquity, but rejoices in the truth; Bears all things, believes all things, hopes all thing, endures all things."

1 Corinthians 13 (NKJV)

My thoughts for today...

If you have love, you have fulfilled all the laws of the Bible. This is the reason why it is crucial to forgive others!

This world can be a very dark place unless we invite Jesus in to guide us along the way.

From Genesis to Revelation, the Bible tells us that "God is with us!"

JESUS THE CORNERSTONE

Jesus is the Rock that holds me secure
As the world comes tumbling down around me.

He is the Anchor that I cling to
When life's crashing waves try to dislodge me,
Pulling me downstream.

But I will not fear;
For when I am weak and I cannot stand
Or when I flounder and I cannot swim
I hold tightly to my Cornerstone!

My thoughts for today…

God doesn't need money to get things done, for God uses people.

As with Job, the Lord will restore the stolen years
that the locusts have eaten--
and give you double for your trouble!

MERCY, NOT SACRIFICE

"Yet I say to you that in this place, there is One greater than the temple. But if you had known what this means, 'I desire *mercy* and not *sacrifice*, you would not have condemned the guiltless.'"

Matthew 12:6-7 (NKJV)

My thoughts for today...

In Hebrew the word for mercy is hesed, which means *steadfast love.*

It is the word zavach in the Hebrew which has the idea of *giving up what is close to your heart to have a relationship with God.*

In short, God desires us to have a steadfast kind of love, and it is not necessary to give up what is closest to our hearts to have a relationship with Him or to please Him.

God loves us so completely and unconditionally already that this is unnecessary and *unwanted!*

It is truly sad that the Jewish religious leaders were

so consumed in their efforts to be righteous by following all the laws that they failed to recognize the arrival of the true Messiah, Jesus Christ, "the One foretold."

REJOICE

"Rejoice in the Lord always. Again I will say, rejoice!"

Philippians 4:4 (NKJV)

My thoughts for today...

Rejoice!: the first word spoken by the angel, Gabriel, sent by God, to announce to the Virgin Mary that she would conceive by the Holy Spirit and give birth to the Messiah.

Rejoice!: the first word spoken by Jesus to the women who were the first to see Him after His resurrection.

The Bible tells us that each time God sent an angel from heaven to give certain people a message, that person then went "in haste" to carry it out, and is there any wonder?!!

THE GOOD SHEPHERD

"I am the good shepherd. The good shepherd gives His life for the sheep."

John 10:11 (NKJV)

My thoughts for today…

Jesus gave His life for me, so I now live my life for Him!

We should be giving praise always, especially during the difficult times, knowing that to those who love God-- He will turn it for our good.

In life, we sometimes take detours which leaves us feeling lost. But God never gives up on us and will keep working with us to get us back on course.

Laughter is a medicine and soothes whatever ails you.

To laugh is to chase away the curse of worry.

Live like there is no tomorrow, for tomorrow is not promised us.

God loves us all—ALL of the time!

JESUS DOES NOT JUDGE

"You judge according to the flesh; I judge no one."

John 8:15 (NKJV)

My thoughts for today...

The Bible portrays how Jesus always made His way directly to those that were downtrodden and mistreated by society, then He often lingered, showing them kindness, compassion, and unconditional love.

God is always doing things which we cannot see; therefore, like walking in the dark-- we will need to go by faith and not by sight, until our hearts' desires appear before us.

Jesus always keeps His promises and He promised to not leave us as orphans but will come to us when we call out to Him. We learn to recognize His voice when we go to Him often, in the good times as well as the bad, as this makes our communication stronger.

What a wonderful God we serve,
for He is the Alpha and the Omega,
the Beginning and the End!

JESUS WAS A GOD-SEND

"Come near to Me, Hear this:

I have not spoken in secret from the beginning;

From the time that I was, I was there.

And now the Lord God and His Spirit have sent Me."

Isaiah 48:16 (NKJV)

"I and My Father are One."

John 10:30 (NKJV)

My thoughts for today…

God's plans are a mystery--for our questions are often met with a period.

Jesus answers every prayer with, "Don't worry, I am with you."

I asked God, "Why all this pain, Lord? Why can't I have a trouble-free life?" But even as I ask, I know—that without it I would not grow or humble myself before You or learn to fully trust You. And this too I know, that this pain is gain.

> I'm putting on a new person
> For I'm no longer a worrier
> But a warrior!

FREE INDEED

"Therefore, if the Son makes you free, you shall be free indeed."

John 8:36 (NKJV)

My thoughts for today…

Going to God with all your problems and all your pain is the only way, for God is the only one that can turn it around.

Better to be strong and courageous than to worry, for worry only leaves us feeling weak and helpless.

Worry avails nothing while faith accomplishes much.

Our hearts magnify the Lord, who hears our cries and the petitions of our hearts. How great is our God!

Why, oh why do we allow our minds to worry when all the time, deep down, we know that God's got this!

God is love; and while you may wonder how God can still love you, God is saying, "How can I *not!*"

God says, "You thought it was over, but it's only *just begun!*"

THE DEVIL IS A LIAR

"Who is a liar but he who denies that Jesus is the Christ?

He is the antichrist who denies the Father and the Son.

Whoever denies the Son does not have the Father either;

He who acknowledges the Son has the Father also."

        1 John 2:22-23 (NKJV)

"By this you know the Spirit of God;

 Every spirit that confesses that Jesus Christ has come in the flesh is of God,

And every spirit that does not confess that Jesus Christ has come in the flesh

is not of God.

And this is the spirit of the Anti-Christ,

Which you have heard is coming,

and is now already in the world."

1 John 4:2-3 (NKJV)

My thoughts for today...

There has been much discussion about the anti-Christ;

however, the Bible tells us clearly, that the "anti-Christ" is actually he who denies that Jesus is the Christ, the Son of God!

Therefore, the Anti-Christ is the *spirit of the unbeliever!*

BORN OF GOD

"Whoever has been born of God *does not sin*,

For His seed remains in him;

And He *cannot sin*,

Because he has been born of God.

                            1 John 3:9 (NKJV)

"In this the children of God and the children of the devil are manifest;

Whoever does not practice righteousness is not of God,

Nor is he who does not love his brother.

For this is the message that you heard from the beginning,

That we should love one another."

                         1 John 3:10-11 (NKJV)

"And now, little children, abide in Him, that when He appears,

We may have confidence and not be ashamed before Him at His coming."

1 John 2:28 (NKJV)

My thoughts for today...

When Jesus comes back on the cloud, as promised, there will be gladness.

But the ones who are ashamed will be the ones that refused to accept Jesus Christ…

and knowing full well, that it is now…too late!

FULFILLMENT OF GOD'S WILL

"Sacrifice and offering You did not *desire*,

But a body You have prepared for Me.

In burnt offerings and sacrifices for sin You had no *pleasure*.

Then I said, 'Behold, I have come—In the volume of the book

It is *written of Me*—To do Your will, O God.'"

                                    Hebrews 10:5-7 (NKJV)

"By that will we have been sanctified through the offering of the body of Jesus Christ *once for all*."

                                    Hebrews 10:10 (NKJV)

"Afterwards God said: "Their sins and their lawless deeds, I will remember *no more.*"

                                    Hebrews 10:10-17 (NKJV)

*desire: want; wish for

*pleasure: a pleased feeling; enjoyment; delight; satisfaction

*once: on one occasion; one time only

*no more: no longer; never again

*Written of Me: Hundreds of Old Testament prophecies in the Bible point to Jesus Christ!

My thoughts for today...

When you approach God, rest assured that He is sitting on His throne of mercy.

God loves us so much that even when we tell Him to go away—*He stays!*

THE WAY, THE TRUTH, AND THE LIFE

"Let not your heart be troubled;

You believe in God,

Believe also in Me.

In My Father's house are many mansions,

If it were not so, I would have told you.

And if I go and prepare a place for you,

I will *come again*. And receive you to Myself.

That where I am,

There you may be also.

And where I go, you know and the way you know.

I am the way, the truth and the life.

No one comes to the Father

Except through Me."

John 14:1-6 (NKJV)

*come again: return

*no one: no person; not a single person

*except: other than; with the exclusion of; apart from

My thoughts for today...

There is only *one* way to the Father and that is through Jesus Christ.

Jesus made this possible when He chose to accept the will of God and willingly died on the Cross so that our sins might be forgiven.

THE PROMISED ONE

"And John bore witness, saying, 'I saw the Spirit descending from heaven like a dove, and He remained upon Him.

I did not know Him, but, Him who sent me to baptize with water, said to me, 'Upon whom you see the Spirit descending, and remaining on Him,

This is He who baptizes with the Holy Spirit.'

And I have seen and testified that this is the Son of God.'"

John 1:32-34 (NKJV)

My thoughts for today...

God gave John the Baptist specific instructions in what to look for to recognize the Christ and to verify His identity, describing how the Holy Spirit would come down and remain on Him. This is how we can also know, without a doubt, that Jesus Christ *is* the Promised One!

The Holy Bible is our treasure chest, filled with the promises of God.

To be an unbeliever is to be a skeptic;

While to be a believer is to have a saving faith.

HATED BY THE WORLD

"If I had not come and spoken to them, they would have no sin,

But now they have no excuse for their sin.

He who hates Me hates My Father also.

If I had not done among them the works which no one else did,

They would have no sin; but now they have seen and also hate both

Me and My Father.

But this happened that the word might be fulfilled which is written

In their law, 'They hated Me without a cause.'"

John 15:22-25 (NKJV)

"Then He said to them, 'O foolish ones, and slow to believe in all that the prophets have spoken!

Ought not the Christ to have suffered these things and to enter into His glory?'"

Luke 24: 25-26 (NKJV)

My thoughts for today...

A prophet has no honor in his own home or hometown, for even though Jesus was following His Father's will, there were doubters. The Jewish leaders doubted Jesus being the Messiah, even after seeing the miracles of healing the sick and lame. Perhaps this is because familiarity breeds contempt, and Jesus tells us that those that follow Him will be treated in the same way, for those who are given a calling will not be believed by their immediate families or people that have known them a long time.

Jesus was the perfect unblemished Lamb
Sent from God to save us from our sins.
Thereby, fulfilling His purpose.

CONFIDENCE IN PRAYER

"Now this is the confidence that we have in Him, that if we ask anything according to His will, He hears us. And if we know that He hears us, whatever we ask, we know that we have the petitions that we have asked of Him."

1 John 5:14-15 (NKJV)

My thoughts for today...

This verse goes back to the time that Jesus told us that we will need to believe as children. For a child's believing is so real to them that it is "knowing!"

Whatever your faith beliefs are, that's fine, as we should all have our own personal relationship with God. However, if your faith focus is not on Jesus and His finished work on the cross, then you are making it all about you—and not about Him. Big mistake! Just saying…

When we come to the end of ourselves, that is when we will feel Jesus' presence the most.

Include God in all that you do. Make Him inclusive in your life. God loves you unconditionally and just as any parent, He wants to share in your activities or whatever you have going on at the moment. Please don't shut Him out!

> You are precious in God's eyes. God looks at you and He sees a rose.
>
> A rose with a sweet-smelling aroma.
>
> All this, because of the finished work of Jesus on the cross.

KNOWING THE TRUE, REJECTING THE FALSE

"We *know* that whoever is born of God does not sin; but he who has been born of God keeps himself, and the wicked one does not touch him.

We *know* that we are of God, and the whole world lies under the sway of the wicked one.

And we *know* that the Son of God has come and has given us an understanding, that we may know Him who is true; and we are in Him who is true, in His Son Jesus Christ. This is the true God and eternal life."

1 John 5:18-20 (NKJV)

"If anyone sees his brother sinning a *sin which does not lead to death*, he will ask, and He will give him life for those who commit sin not leading to death. There *is* sin leading to death. I do not say that he should pray about that. All unrighteousness is sin, and there is sin *not* leading to death."

1 John 5:16-17 (NKJV)

My thoughts for today...

We sin every single day of our lives, but these sins do not lead to death (not having eternal life).

However, to not believe that Jesus Christ is the Son of God and not accept Him into our hearts IS the ultimate sin which leads to death (not having eternal life);

For Jesus is the Way, the Truth, and the *Life!*

God is love, and you are His child, His child that He loves *unconditionally.* When you let this sink in, each day of the rest of your life will be your best life yet!

OBEDIENCE BY FAITH

"If someone says, 'I love God,' and hates his brother, he is a liar; for he who does not love his brother whom he has seen, how can he love God whom he has not seen? And this commandment we have from Him: that he who loves God *must* love his brother also."

1 John 4:20-21 (NKJV)

"Whoever believes that Jesus is the Christ is born of God, and everyone who loves Him who begot also loves him who is begotten of Him.

1 John 5:1 (NKJV)

"For whatever is born of God overcomes the world. And this is the victory that has overcome the world—our faith. Who is he who overcomes the world, but he who believes that Jesus is the Son of God?

1 John 5:4-5 (NKJV)

"And we have known and believed the love that God has for us. God is love, and he who abides in love abides in God, and God in him."

1 John 4:16 (NKJV)

My thoughts for today…

I believe that anyone just beginning their spiritual journey would do well to begin reading their Bibles starting with the Book of John.

It has been said that John is the disciple that Jesus loved the most. And while that point might be debatable, as you read his gospel, it is evident that John spent a lot of time hanging on to Jesus' every word, truly soaking up His teachings….and thereby, the nature of His love.

THE GREAT AND AWESOME DAY OF THE LORD

"And it shall come to pass

That whoever calls upon the name of the Lord

Shall be saved."

Acts 2:21 (NKJV)

My thoughts for today...

As the Lord opens my eyes to the many wonders around me

Poetry spurts from deep within my soul!

I am but a broken piece of humanity forever loved by God!

I am happy because Jesus loves me. I am strong because God is with me.

The Lord comes to us in our distress and cleans up our mess.

God leans down from His mighty throne, in all His

holiness, to whisper words of love and encouragement in our ears, forever leaving us in awe and wonder.

Jesus is our King, as well as our Savior; thus, because we are all children of God, this makes you and me-- a prince or princess!

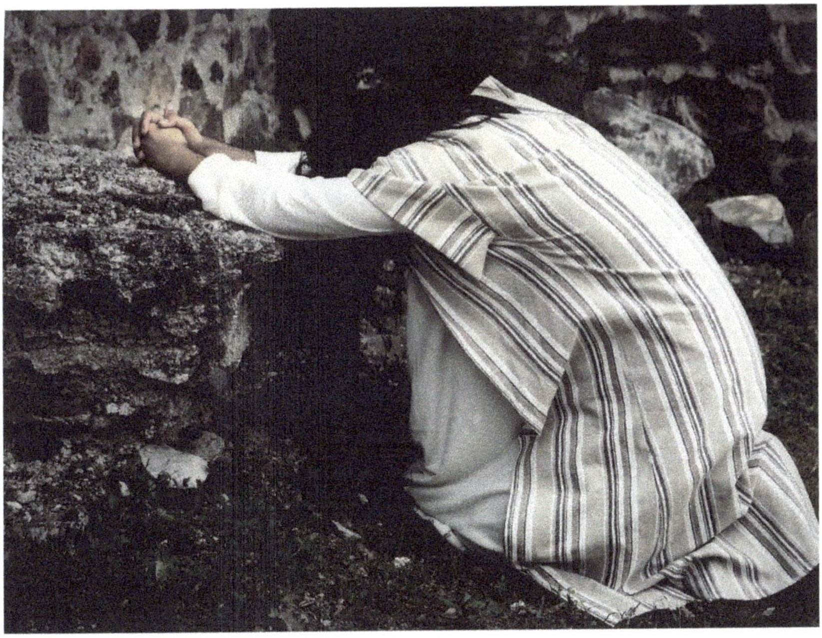

JESUS PRAYING IN THE GARDEN

"Coming out, Jesus went to the Mount of Olives, as He was accustomed.

And His disciples also followed Him.

When He came to the place, He said to them,

'Pray that you do not enter into temptation.'

And He was withdrawn from them about a stone's throw,

And He knelt down and prayed, saying

'Father, if it is Your will, take this cup away from Me,

Nevertheless, Not My will, but Yours be done.'

Then an angel appeared to Him from heaven, strengthening Him,

And being in agony, He prayed more earnestly.

Then His sweat became like great drops of blood falling down to the ground.

When He rose up from prayer, and had come to His disciples,

He found them sleeping from *sorrow.*

Then He said to them, 'Why do you sleep? Rise and pray,

Lest you enter into temptation.'"

Luke 22:39-45 (NKJV)

*sorrow: a deep distress, sadness, or regret especially for the loss of someone or something loved

---

My thoughts for today…

There has been much discussion concerning Jesus' disciples falling asleep while Jesus was praying in the garden, while occasionally expressing fault. However, the Bible clearly tells us that they slept, because their hearts were heavy, *from the sorrow* in knowing that He would soon be leaving them. So, in reality, His disciples were sleeping because they were feeling exhausted and drained from their sadness.

ANOINTING OF JESUS' FEET

"Then Mary took a pound of very costly oil of spikenard,

anointed the feet of Jesus, and wiped His feet with her hair.

And the house was filled with the fragrance of the oil.

But one of His disciples, Judas Iscariot, Simon's son, who would betray Him, said,

"Why was this fragrant oil not sold for three hundred denarii and given to the poor?" This he said, not that he cared for the poor, but because he was a thief, and had the money box; and he used to take what was put in it.

But Jesus said,

"Let her alone; she has kept this for the day of My burial.

For the poor you have with you always, but Me you do not have always."

John 12:3-7 (NKJV)

My thoughts for today...

When Jesus was born, the three wise men brought him gold, frankincense, and myrrh.

Then shortly before Jesus' death, a pound of very costly oil of spikenard was poured upon His feet.

For, although Jesus' purpose in life was to give His life for ours, God did not withhold showing honor to His beloved Son.

So, rest assured, God will not withhold honor from you either!

CAIAPHAS PROPHESIED CONCERNING JESUS

"Then many of the Jews who had come to Mary,

And had seen the things that Jesus did, believed in Him.

But some of them went away to the Pharisees and told them the things Jesus did.

Then the chief priests and the Pharisees gathered a council and said,

"What shall we do? For this Man works many signs.

If we let Him alone like this, everyone will believe in Him,

And the Romans will come and take away both our place and nation."

And one of them, Caiaphas, being high priest that year, said to them,

'You know nothing at all, nor do you consider

That it is expedient for us that for the people, one man should die for the people,

And not that the whole nation should perish.'

Now he prophesied that Jesus would die for the nation,

And not for that nation only, but also that,

He would gather together in one,

The children of God, who were scattered abroad."

John 11:45-52 (NKJV)

My thoughts for today…

Most things in life contain a certain level of politics; thus, regarding Jesus and His teachings, this was no exception. For politics played a major role in the reason that the chief priests and the Pharisees wanted to do away with Jesus.

For they feared that if everyone believed in Jesus, the Romans would remove them from office and dissolve the Jewish nation.

JESUS RAISED LAZARUS FROM THE DEAD

"Then Jesus, again groaning in Himself, came to the tomb.

It was a cave, and a stone lay against it. Jesus said, 'Take away the stone.'

Martha, the sister of him who was dead, said to Him,

'Lord, by this time there is a stench, for he has been dead four days.'

Jesus said to her, 'Did I not say that if you would believe, you would see the glory of God?'

Then they rolled away the stone from the place where the dead man was lying.

And Jesus lifted up His eyes and said,

'Father, I thank You that You have heard Me.

And I know that You always hear Me, but because of the people who are

Standing by I said this, that they may believe that You sent Me.'

Now when He had said these things, He cried with a loud voice,

'Lazarus, come forth!'

And he who had died came out bound hand and foot with graveclothes,

And his face was wrapped with a cloth.

Jesus said to them, "Loose him, and let him go."

John 11:38-44 (NKJV)

My thoughts for today…

JESUS CAME TO FREE THE CAPTIVES!

When Jesus raised Lazarus from the dead, we understand the meaning at a physical level, but it has a deeper meaning; for in effect, it is showing us that Jesus loosens not only our physical but also our emotional burdens as well. And afterwards—we are left feeling free!

PLOT TO KILL LAZARUS

"Now a great many of the Jews knew that He was there,

and they came, not for Jesus' sake only, but that they might also see Lazarus,

whom He had raised from the dead. But the chief priests plotted to put Lazarus to death also, because on account of him, many of the Jews went away, and believed in Jesus."

John 12:9-11 (NKJV)

My thoughts for today…

One of the greatest miracles that Jesus ever did was raising his friend,

Lazarus, from the dead; for this was the focal turning point, in which many believed in Jesus.

The people saw for themselves Lazarus: alive, well, and walking among them, which provided substantial proof that Jesus had been given power and authority from God.

In everything we are to be grateful, for even in the bad, we can find some good.

God pulls us out of the mud holes-- even the ones we dug ourselves.

Jesus brings dead things back to life,

including our barren dreams!

JESUS RODE A LOWLY DONKEY INTO JERUSALEM

"The next day a great multitude that had come to the feast,

When they heard that Jesus was coming to Jerusalem,

Took branches of palm trees and went out to meet Him, and cried out:

'Hosanna!' 'Blessed is He who comes in the name of the Lord!'

'The King of Israel!'

Then, Jesus, when He had found a young donkey, sat on it.

As it is written:

'Fear not, daughter of Zion;

Behold, your King is coming, sitting on a donkey's colt.'

His disciples did not understand these things at first;

But when Jesus was glorified,

Then they remembered that these things were written about Him,

And that they had done these things to Him."

John 12:12-16 (NKJV)

My thoughts for today…

Jesus was glorified in His resurrection for the glorification of His Father.

The miracle of the woman that had the issue of blood and who touched the hem of Jesus' garment is that, in effect, she was actually kissing the hem of God's garment!

Forget about getting even—
For two wrongs don't make a right!

DO NOT WEEP FOR ME

"Now as they led Jesus away, they laid hold of a certain man,

Simon, a Cyrenian, who was coming from the country.

And on him they laid the cross that he might bear it after Jesus.

And a great multitude of the people followed Him.

And women who also mourned and lamented Him.

But Jesus, turning to them, said,

'Daughters of Jerusalem, do not weep for Me,

But weep for yourselves and for your children.

For indeed the days are coming in which they will say,

'Blessed are the barren, wombs that never bore,

And breast which never nursed!'

Then they will begin to say to the mountains,

'Fall on us!' and to the hills, 'Cover us!'

For if they do these things in the green wood, what will be done in the dry?'"

Luke 23:26-31 (NKJV)

My thoughts for today...

In the last days, mothers will fear for their children, for there will be great trouble and anguish upon the land.

Numbing fear largely comes from fear itself,

And is, more often than not, the fear of the possibility

And not of the actually!

PARADISE

"The soldiers also mocked Him, coming and offering Him sour wine, and saying,

'If you are the King of the Jews, save Yourself!'

And an inscription also was written over Him in Greek, Latin, and Hebrew:

THIS IS THE KING OF THE JEWS.

Then one of the criminals who were hanged blasphemed Him, saying,

'If You are the Christ, save Yourself and us.'

But the other, answering, rebuked him, saying, 'Do you not even fear God,

Seeing you are under the same condemnation? And we indeed justly, for we receive the due reward of our deeds, but this Man has done nothing wrong."

Then he said to Jesus, 'Lord, remember me when You come into Your kingdom.'

And Jesus said to him, 'Assuredly, I say to you, today you will be with Me in Paradise.'"

Luke 23:36-43 (NKJV)

My thoughts for today...

The children of God will one day be with their Heavenly Father in Paradise (heaven), where they will be filled to the brim with happiness and a joyful peace!

When troubles come and the future looks uncertain, let's not forget about our God, who can do all things!

God did not promise us a rose garden in this life but He *did* promise us a paradise in the next!

CAUGHT UP INTO PARADISE

"I know a man in Christ who fourteen years ago—

Whether in the body I do not know, or whether out of the body,

I do not know, God knows—

Such a one was caught up to the third heaven.

And I know such a man—whether in the body or out of the body,

I do not know, God knows—

How he was caught up into Paradise and heard inexpressible words,

Which it is not lawful for a man to utter."

2 Corinthians 12:2-4 (NKJV)

"He who has an ear, let him hear what the Spirit says to the churches.

To him who overcomes I will give to eat from the tree of life, which is in the midst of the Paradise of God."

Revelation 2:7 (NKJV)

My thoughts for today…

There are many names to describe God, but oftentimes, the most

important one is overlooked; for the Bible tells us, God is *love!*

The reason I love the Holy Bible as my point of reference is that the Old Testament is telling us about God's plan that will one day unfold to give us salvation, while, the New Testament testifies of this having been accomplished in Jesus Christ, the Son of God, by His sacrifice on the Cross.

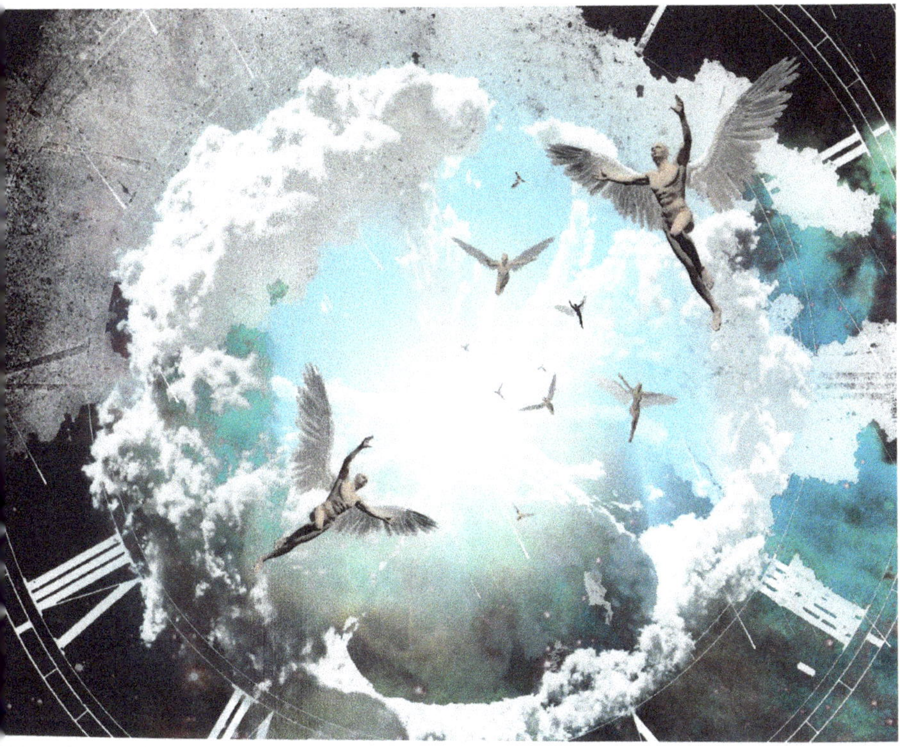

GUARDIAN ANGELS

"Because you have made the Lord, who is my *refuge*, even the Most High, your dwelling place, no evil shall befall you, nor any plague come near your dwelling.

For He shall give His angels *charge* over you, to *keep* you in all your ways."
Psalm 91:9-11 (NKJV)

"And she saw two angels in white sitting, one at the head and the other at the feet, where the body of Jesus had lain."
John 20:12 (NKJV)

"Do not forget to entertain strangers, for by so doing some have unwittingly entertained angels."
Hebrews 13:2 (NKJV)

*refuge: shelter or protection from danger or distress

*charge: entrust (someone) with a task or responsibility

*keep: to watch over and defend; to take care of

My thoughts for today...

Angels are mentioned many times in the Bible, as they play an important role in the heavenly ream, with God using them as messengers and guardians, among other duties. What's more, God's angels are surrounding us even now, here on earth; just because we cannot see them makes them no less there. In fact, at our birth, God assigns each one of us our very own guardian angel, who stays with us our entire lifetime.

As the butterflies soar and dip across the earthly sky,
So do the angels in their heavenly spire!

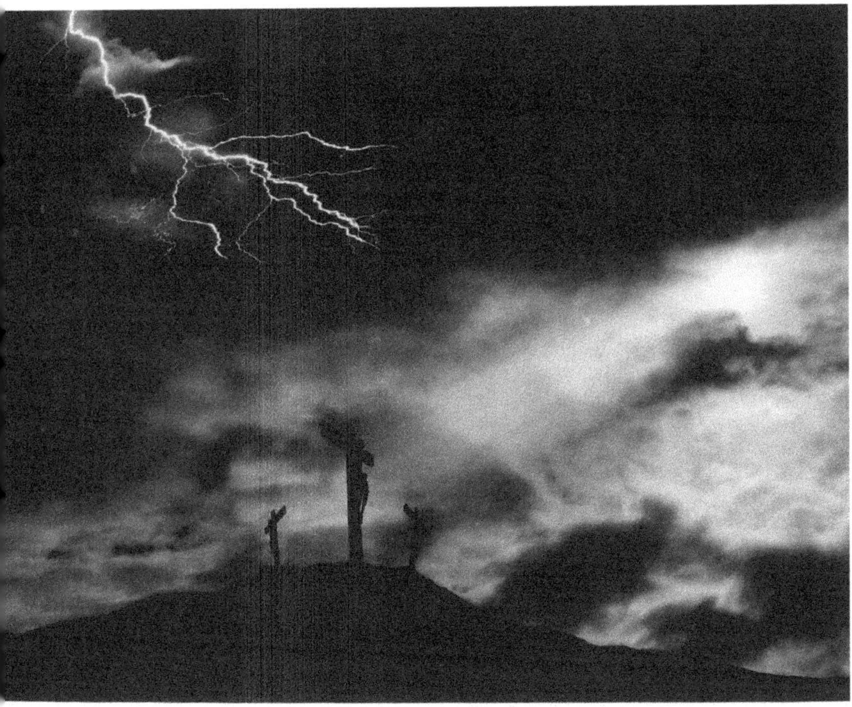

JESUS FULFILLED HIS DESTINY

While some people do the talk, Jesus did the walk, by going to the cross to die for our sins. Furthermore, Jesus did this afraid, for we glimpse the anguish He felt, while praying in the Garden of Gethsemane, where His sweat turned to drops of blood, stemming from His anxiety of knowing what lay ahead of Him. While praying, Jesus asked His Father if this could be removed from Him, but ultimately Jesus finished His prayer with, *'Not My will, but Your will be done."*

Shortly afterwards, Jesus was arrested and sentenced to die by means of *crucifixion*, but first, Jesus was severely *flogged*.

Subsequently, the flogging left Jesus in a weakened condition; therefore, He stumbled as He walked toward the place where He would be crucified. Adding to this was the fact that Jesus' eyes were almost swollen shut, and blood dripped down His forehead and ran into His eyes from where a crown of thorns had been forcefully shoved upon His head, making it difficult to see in front of Him.

Nevertheless, Jesus peered through the slits of His

eyes, His breathing labored and His body full of pain, and kept going forward, stumbling as He went.

After His crucifixion, the soldiers removed Jesus' lifeless body from the cross. As they lifted Him down, His limp body fell into the arms of the three women below.

To gaze at His face was heartbreaking, for His face was still etched with the exhaustion and agony that He had endured while on the cross.

Yet it was finished, for Jesus had fulfilled His purpose in life and willingly given His life on the cross, thereby, affirming His love for His Heavenly Father and *mankind*.

The crucifixion of Jesus Christ emphasizes the sacrifice on the Cross and the victory over death.

*crucifixion: a method of capital punishment in which the victim is tied or nailed to a large wooden cross or beam and left to hang until eventual death.

*flogged: punishment of hitting someone with a whip; beating; scourging

*mankind: universe; man; all of the living human inhabitants of the earth

BLESSED BY BELIEVING

"Now Thomas, called the Twin, one of the twelve, was not with them when Jesus came. The other disciples therefore said to him, 'We have seen the Lord.'

So, he said to them, 'Unless I see in His hands the print of the nails, and put my hand into His side, I will not believe.'

And after eight days His disciples were again inside, and Thomas with them.

Jesus came, the doors being shut, and stood in the midst, and said,

'Peace to you!'

Then He said to Thomas, 'Reach your finger here, and look at My hands, and reach your hand here, and put it into My side.

Do not be <u>unbelieving</u>, but <u>believing</u>.'

And Thomas answered and said to Him, 'My Lord and my God!'

Jesus said to him, 'Thomas, because you have

seen Me, you have believed.

Blessed are those who have not seen and yet have believed.'"

John 20:24-29 (NKJV)

"And truly, Jesus did many other signs in the presence of His disciples, which are not written in this book, but these are written that you may believe that Jesus is the Christ, the Son of God. And that believing you may have life in His name."

John 20:30-31 (NKJV)

My thoughts for today...

The word, "Amen," is derived from the Hebrew amen, meaning "certainty" and "verify," which means "*so be it!*"

PROMISE OF THE FATHER

"And being assembled together with them, He commanded them not to depart from Jerusalem, but to wait for the Promise of the Father, 'which,' He said, 'you have heard from Me; for John truly baptized with water, but you shall be baptized with the Holy Spirit not many days from now.'"

Acts 1:4-5 (NKJV)

"But you shall receive power when the Holy Spirit has come upon you, and you shall be witnesses to Me in Jerusalem, and in all Judea and Samaria, and to the ends of the earth."

Acts 1:8 (NKJV)

"Now when He had spoken these things, while they watched, He was *taken up*, and a cloud received Him out of their sight. And while they looked steadfastly toward heaven as He went up, behold, two men stood by them in white apparel, who also said, 'Men of Galilee, why do you stand gazing up into heaven? This same Jesus, who was taken up from you into heaven, will so come *in like manner* as you saw Him go into heaven.'"

Acts 1:9-11 (NKJV)

*taken up: uplifted or elevated

*in like manner: again; likewise

My thoughts for today...

Hear ye hear ye...To him who has an ear, hear this--
Ready or not! Jesus is coming back!

We are all God's children;
and while it is good to love God and put Him first,
It is vital to realize just how much God loves *us!*

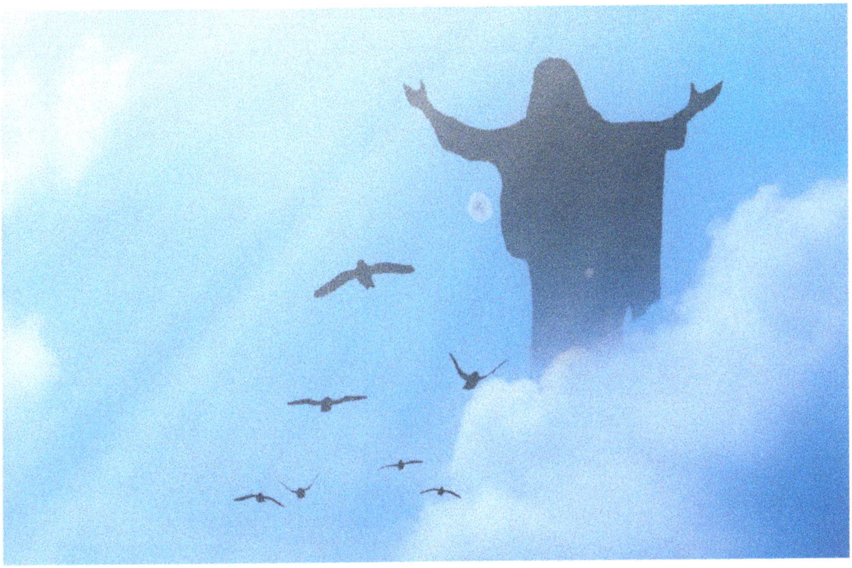

WHEN JESUS RETURNS

"Immediately after the tribulation of those days, the sun will be darkened and the moon will not give its light. The stars will fall from heaven, and the powers of the heavens will be shaken. Then the sign of the Son of Man will appear in heaven and then all the tribes of the earth will mourn and they will see the Son of Man coming on the clouds of heaven with power and great glory.

And He will send His angels with a great sound of a trumpet and they will gather together His elect from the four winds, from one end of heaven to the other."

Matthew 24:29-31 (NKV)

My thoughts for today…

When Jesus appears in the sky, on a large cloud that spreads long and wide,

His arrival will be accompanied by a great howling, turbulent wind caused by the four winds coming together from the ends of the earth (the angry howling winds sound similar to when Jesus was hanging on the cross),

which will strike fear and dread into the hearts of all those who have not accepted Jesus Christ into their hearts.

But those who have accepted Jesus will be filled with a gladness, mixed with awe, as they are swept up upon the cloud by His accompaniment of angels, to stand just behind Jesus, as they look on-- at all the things that are taking place around them.

JESUS EXALTED ABOVE THE ANGELS

"God, who at various times and in various ways, spoke in time past to the fathers by prophets, has in these last days spoken to us by His Son, whom He has appointed *heir* of all things, through whom He made the worlds, Who being the brightness of His glory and the express image of His person, and upholding all things by the word of His power, when He had by Himself *purged* our sins, sit down at the right hand of the Majesty on High, having become so much better than the angels, as He has by inheritance obtained a more excellent name than they."

Hebrews 1:1-4 (NKJV)

"For when we were still without strength, in due time Christ died for the ungodly."

Romans 5:6 (NKJV)

*heir: a person legally entitled to property

*purged: to make clean; cleanse; purify

My thoughts for today...

Jesus said that in this world we would have tribulation, but He has overcome the world. So, keep your focus on Him and you will overcome too!

If we are to love like Jesus, we will need to love without conditions or boundaries!

Jesus is with us always—even during the slipping and sliding of our mistakes.

Nothing can compare with the peace of Jesus—
For it is a peace that surpasses understanding.

HOPE DOES NOT DISAPPOINT

"Now hope does not disappoint, because the love of God has been poured out in our hearts by the Holy Spirit who was given to us."

Romans 5:5 (NKJV)

"This hope, we have as an anchor of the soul, both sure and steadfast, and which enters the Presence behind the veil, where the forerunner has entered for us, even Jesus, having become High Priest forever according to the order of Melchizedek."

Hebrews 6:19-20 (NKJV)

My thoughts for today…

To obey God is like jumping off a tall building, for you flail your arms and flap your wings, trying to increase altitude in the middle of your freefall.

Then your faith kicks in like a parachute, and trustworthy God helps you to land uprightly and unashamedly, with your feet softly touching the ground.

As the world changes and opportunities dwindle, you might look around, feeling confused, wondering where God is in all of this.

However, God is still in control and trusting God, a lot of times, means to just keep going forward, with eyes in front of you, not looking to the left or to the right, because you know that God has your back.

Put your trust in God and never give up hope,
And watch Him do the impossible;
Setting you up to succeed past your wildest dreams!

SWEET-SMELLING AROMA

"Therefore be imitators of God as dear children. And walk in love, as Christ also has loved us and given Himself for us, an offering and a sacrifice to God for a sweet-smelling aroma."

Ephesians 5:1-2 (NKJV)

My thoughts for today…

It is my goal to impart to our youth how much God loves them. And for the young ladies who have been told that you are the weaker sex, this pertains only to muscular strength. Ultimately, this does not make you inferior. For females are just as much children of God as males, as we are "all" children of God.

God is love and He does not show partiality; in His eyes, being a female, you are "equally' loved. So, ladies, hold your heads up with your shoulders back, not haughtily, but with full confidence that you are a child of God and fully loved.

You are God's beautiful flower,
Even with all of your flaws;
For there is no flaw that could ever stop
your sweet aroma from reaching the nostrils
of your loving Father in heaven!

MY CUP RUNNETH OVER

"You prepare a table before me in the presence of my enemies;

You anoint my head with oil. My cup runs over.

Surely goodness and mercy shall follow me all the days of my life;

And I shall dwell in the house of the Lord forever."

Psalm 23:5-6 (NKJV)

My thoughts for today…

God's love is unconditional; so, it matters not, if you are the victim-- or the bully.

He loves us all, so He will not help you by getting even with your enemies.

Instead, God will lovingly promote you in *front* of your enemies!

Loving others is not always easy.

Nonetheless, it is a commandment.

Let it go-- beginning each new day as if you had never been hurt!

FEARLESS

"Yea, though I walk through the valley of the shadow of death,

I will fear no evil; for You are with me;

Your rod and Your staff, they comfort me."

Psalm 23:4 (NKJV)

My thoughts for today...

Whether it be in this life-- or the next, the Lord is always "with us!"

In *everything* we are to be grateful-- for to those that love God, He will take the bad and use it for our good!

While people's love can be a bit shaky—God's love is unwavering.

Love is oft better shown than said.

.Keep going forward and let the chips fall where they may!

MY LORD, MY SHEPHERD

"The Lord is my shepherd; I shall not want.

He makes me to lie down in green pastures;

He leads me beside the still waters.

He restores my soul; He leads me in the paths of righteousness

for His name's sake."

Psalm 23:1-3 (NKJV)

My thoughts for today...

The Lord provides for us-- leading and guiding us, thus giving us direction in all that we do.

Our dreams tend to look like scattered bits of paper,
blown away by the wind;
But by faith, we can see God
capturing our tattered book of dreams;
gathering them from the four corners of the earth,
and putting all the pieces back together--
while breathing life back into each and every chapter!

KNOWING GOD

"Beloved, let us love one another,
For love is of God;
And everyone who loves is of God
And knows God.
He who does not love
Does not know God,
For God *is* love."

                                              1 John 4:7-8 (NKJV)

"If someone says, 'I love God,'
And hates his brother,
He is a liar,
For he who does not love his brother whom he has seen,
How can he love God whom he has not seen?
And this commandment we have from Him;
That he who loves God *must* love his brother also."

                                            1 John 4:20-21 (NKJV)

My thoughts for today...

The Bible clearly tells us: To love is to *know God.*
What a beautiful thought!

THE GOOD NEWS

"Then Jesus said to those Jews who believed Him, 'If you *abide* in My *word*,

You are My disciples indeed. And you shall know the truth, and the truth shall set you free.'"

John 8:31-32 (NKJV)

*abide: (accept; to remain in, constant existing)

*word: (news or information; verbal signal, password)

"And He said to them, 'You are from beneath, I am from above. You are of this world; I am not of this world. Therefore I said to you that you will die in your sins; for if you do not believe that I am *He*, you will die in your sins.'"

John 8:23-24 (NKJV)

My thoughts for today...

For no one is without sin—however, when we choose to abide (accept) in Jesus' word (news), this sets us free.

What is this news? Jesus tells us that by accepting

Him into our hearts, believing that He is the Son of God, and has already paid the price for our sins, this unloads our burden of sin.

It is this knowledge and belief, that God loves us unconditionally and that His Son, Jesus Christ, willingly gave His life on the Cross (once for all), to cleanse us of our sins, that allows us to live a freedom-filled life.

We will only need to believe to receive—it's that simple!

And this is why the gospel of Jesus Christ is called, "The Good News!"

THE KINGDOM BELONGS TO THE LORD

"All of the ends of the world shall remember and turn to the Lord.

And all the families of the nations shall worship before You.

For the kingdom is the Lord's, and He rules over the nations."

Psalm 22:27-28 (NKJV)

My thoughts for today…

Lifting up God in prayer lifts up our own spirits as well.

The Bible is chock full of love and romance, with some of the greatest love stories of all time, such as Solomon and his doe-eyed bride, Boaz and Ruth, Jacob and Rachel, Joseph and Mary, just to name a few!

Showing love in the face of diversity weakens the hold of hatred.

I choose to overlook others' offences because God overlooks mine.

I love God, for God first loved me!

TEMPTATION

"The devil never gives up sending us temptations to sin."

Luke 4:13 (NKJV)

"Then Jesus, being filled with the Holy Spriit, returned from Jordan and was led by the Spirit into the wilderness, being tempted for forty days by the devil. For in those days, He ate nothing, and afterward, when they had ended, He was hungry."

Luke 4:1-2 (NKJV)

"Now when the devil had ended every temptation, he departed from Him until an opportune time."

Luke 4:13 (NKJV)

My thoughts for today...

The enemy tells us that we have made too many mistakes but God says--

That's just another lie!

The path on our journey is long and narrow and it closely follows the mountains that we must climb.

Satan never gives up trying to tempt us to worry and feel condemned,

but we have the victory through the blood of Jesus Christ, so we can say,

"NOT TODAY, SATAN!'

FOLLOW ME

"After these things He came out and saw a tax collector named Levi, sitting at the tax office. And He said to him, 'Follow Me.' So, *he left all*, rose up, and followed Him. Then Levi gave Him a great feast in his own house. And there were a great number of tax collectors and others who sit down with Him. And the Scribes and the Pharisees complained against His disciples, saying, 'Why do You eat and drink with tax collectors and sinners?' Jesus answered and said to them, 'Those who are well have no need for a physician, but those who are sick. I have not come to call the righteous, but sinners to repentance.'"

Luke 5:27-32 (NKJV)

My thoughts for today…

When you have been rejected, it's time to go to Jesus to be accepted!

If we do not make allowances for others, our own mistakes will be magnified.

Waking up to optimism is easy; however, to not allow pessimism in during the day is hard.

While it is human to err, to try to get it right is to our gain.

A battle of the mind is constantly waring inside each of us, and we gain the victory upon releasing the negative thoughts.

When asking a petition in prayer, patience is needed
For God's timing is everything!

IT IS FINISHED

"After this, Jesus knowing that all things were now accomplished, that the Scripture might be fulfilled, said, 'I thirst!'

Now a vessel of sour wine was sitting there; and they filled a sponge with sour wine, put it on hyssop, and put it to His mouth.

So, when Jesus had received the sour wine He said, 'It is *finished!*'

And bowing His head, He gave up His spirit."

John 19:28-30 (NKJV)

*finished: (tetelestai) meaning: the work is complete, in Greek

When Jesus cried out, "It is finished!" on the Cross, the Greek word used is "tetelestai," which means to bring to a close, to complete, to fulfil.

My thoughts for today...

You are precious in God's eyes. God looks at you and

He sees perfection.

All this, because of the finished work of Jesus on the Cross!

When you are secure in God's love, what others think of you become less and less important.

HOPE IN THE LORD

"Be of good courage, and He shall strengthen your heart, all you who hope in the Lord."
Psalm 31:24 (NKJV)

"Let all the earth fear the Lord; let all the inhabitants of the world stand in awe of Him. For He spoke, and it was done; He commanded, and it stood fast."
Psalm 33:8-9 (NKJV)

"Delight yourself also in the Lord, and He shall give you the desires of your heart."
Psalm 36:4 (NKJV)

"Commit your way to the Lord, trust also in Him, and He shall bring it to pass."
Psalm 36:5 (NKJV)

My thoughts for today...

Even before God brings a long-awaited dream to pass,

He has already instilled new dreams into our hearts. And this is because He wants us to keep going forward...

And to live, live, live!

SET FREE

"And you shall know the truth and the truth shall set you free."

John 8:32 (NKJV)

My thoughts for today...

The truth is that we are all children of God.

The truth is that our heavenly Father loves us unconditionally.

The truth is that God loves us so much that He gave His only begotten Son, Jesus Christ, the perfect Lamb, to die for our sins.

The truth is that by accepting Jesus into our hearts, believing that He is the Son of God, we are forgiven and assured of eternal life.

To know *the truth* (that He loves us without conditions) gives us *the freedom* to live without guilt or condemnation.

* the truth: the real facts about something (according to Webster's dictionary) *the freedom: state of being free, liberation from slavery

---

We, as human beings, may bicker and have strife; this is actually the product of Satan. However, we can stay in peace in the midst of the turmoil when we realize that our Creator and Redeemer, God Almighty, is constantly at work and fights our battles for us. So, trust in Him, for God always wins.

God knows each of us by name,
Even the shortened name given to us by our families,
Which shows just how intimate God's love truly is!

GOD CAN DO THE IMPOSSIBLE

"So, when Jesus heard these things, He said to him, 'You still lack one thing. Sell all that you have and distribute to the poor, and you will have treasure in heaven; and come, follow Me.' But when he heard this, he became very sorrowful, for he was very rich.

When Jesus saw that he became sorrowful, He said, 'How hard it is for those who have riches to enter the kingdom of God! For it is easier for a camel to go through the eye of a needle than for a rich man to enter the kingdom of God.'

And those who heard I said, 'Who then can be saved?'

But He said, 'The things which are impossible with men are possible with God.'"

Luke 18:24-27 (NKJV)

"Call to Me, and I will show you great and mighty things, which you do not know."

Jeremiah 33:3 (NKJV)

"For God has not given us a spirit of fear, but of power and of love and of a sound mind."

2 Timothy 1:7 (NKJV)

My thoughts for today...

We tend to start feeling dejected when things are not happening as quickly as we would like, but when we put our trust in God, and are willing to wait on His timing, we can relax, knowing that He will work everything out for our good.

Life is all about the timing, for our years are but seconds to God, and our times are in His hands!

THE ALPHA AND OMEGA

"Father, I desire that they also whom You gave Me,

May be with Me where I am,

That they may behold Your glory which You have given to Me;

For You loved Me *before* the *foundation* of the world."

John 17:24 (NKJV)

*before: earlier than the time or event mentioned

*foundation: a body or ground upon which something is built up or overlaid'

My thoughts for today…

Jesus Christ is God's beloved Son, the perfect Lamb, that came to save the souls of many.

We may search for a miracle; however, Jesus is by far our greatest Miracle.

We know that God loves us and we know that we love God; the rest we can only imagine.

God says simply: Believe to Receive!

JESUS IS BOTH LORD AND CHRIST

"For David did not ascend into the heavens, but he says himself:

'The Lord said to my Lord, sit at My right hand,

Til I make Your enemies Your footstool.'

Therefore, let all the house of Israel know assuredly that God has

Made this Jesus, whom you crucified, both Lord and Christ.'"

Acts 2:34-36 (NKJV)

My thoughts for today…

God throws us an oar when we find ourselves sinking into the depths of despair.

Jesus gives us a pure love that is unconditional, while religions often give us a love that is based entirely upon our performance.

Although you are my brother or sister in Christ, that in no way gives you the right to download your negativity on me, thereby stealing my joy.

Undoubtedly, God gave David the gift of prophesy, in that he foretold tasty morsels concerning Jesus Christ.

And if the truth be told, Jesus is even now sitting at the right hand of God!

GOD IS LONG-SUFFERING

"What man of you, having a hundred sheep, if he loses one of them, does not leave the ninety-nine in the wilderness, and go after the one which is lost until he finds it? And when he has found it, he lays it on his shoulders, rejoicing."

Luke 15:4-5 (NKJV)

"The Lord is not slow to fulfill His promise, as some count slackness, but is longsuffering toward us, not willing that any should perish but that all should come to repentance."

2 Peter 3:9 (NKJV)

My thoughts for today...

Many believe that life will continue on as it has always done.

But this is not the case.

For this world will eventually disappear, because this world is only our temporary home, and God will provide us a perfect world as our permanent home.

Indeed, God loves us so much that He will never give up on us.

Therefore, God calls ministers, teachers, and missionaries to spread the good news of Jesus Christ throughout the earth-- and then the end will come.

JESUS LAY DOWN HIS LIFE

"Therefore, My Father loves Me, because I lay down My life that I may take it up again."

John 10:17 (NKJV)

My thoughts for today…

Jesus left us these loving instructions: "Do not worry, for I am with you."

Simply stated, this world has nothing that can equal our daily walk with God.

We live and breathe, simply because God breathed life into us.

Heading up to heaven, so hand me my harp, because I don't want to be empty handed when I meet my Jesus!

How dare I be sad, for my heart is overflowing with God's goodness.

Broken dreams are actually new beginnings!

MEDITATION

"Finally, brethren, whatever things are true,

Whatever things are noble,

Whatever things are just,

Whatever things are pure,

Whatever things are lovely,

Whatever things are of a good report,

If there is any virtue

And if there is anything praiseworthy—

Meditate on these things."

Philippians 4:8 (NKJV)

My thoughts for today...

Simply, we are to begin our meditations by giving praise and thinking only good thoughts.

Being nice is helpful but being kind is a necessity.

There is only one thing that can turn this world around and that is love.

I thought my life was coming to an end. But when I reached the crossroad,

God placed a bridge there for me to walk over instead!

JOHN THE BAPTIST PREPARES THE WORLD

"I indeed baptize you with water unto repentance, but He who is coming after me is mightier than I, whose sandals I am not worthy to carry.

He will baptize you with the Holy Spirit and fire."

Matthew 3:11 (NKJV)

"For this is He who was spoken of by the prophet Isaiah, saying: 'The voice of one crying in the wilderness.': 'Prepare the way of the Lord, and make His paths straight.'"

Matthew 3:3 (NKJV)

My thoughts for today...

John the Baptist was actually the cousin of Jesus Christ, for John was the son of Elizabeth, the elderly cousin of Mary (the mother of Jesus).

In her youth, Elizabeth was barren, never being able

to have children.

But God saves the best for last, and she later gave birth to a baby boy,

a child blessed by God, whose purpose in life was to announce the soon-coming Messiah, the Christ.

FISHER OF MEN

"So, when they had eaten breakfast, Jesus said to Simon Peter,

'Simon, son of Jonah, do you love Me more than these?'

He said to Him, 'Yes, Lord, You know that I love You.'

He said to him, 'Feed my lambs.'

He said to him a second time, 'Simon, son of Jonah, do you love Me?'

He said, 'Yes Lord, You know that I love You.'

He said to him, 'Feed My sheep.'"

John 21:15-16 (NKJV)

My thoughts for today…

To be secure in God's love is knowing that He will never leave you, no matter what you do or what you say-- or even what you think.

Lord, please give me a faith, with a trust in You, that when You tell me to jump, with no hesitation, I reply:

"How high, O Lord, how high!"

Stop trying to figure it all out, and just *Be!*

WHERE ARE YOU, LORD?

"The Lord is near to all who call upon Him, to all who call upon Him in truth."

Psalm 145:18 (NKJV)

My thoughts for today…

When Jesus was dying on the Cross, at one point He asked God,

"My God, My God, why have you forsaken Me?"

How many of us have asked that same thing at times?

We often feel God has forgotten all about us; however, God is still in control,

And what we are going through is a necessary ingredient, for we cannot produce the end result without going through the process.

I keep doing the things I have always done while waiting for God to do a new thing in my life!

Our personal relationship with God gets deeper and sweeter as the years go by.

Faith is believing that God loves you.
Trust is knowing that God loves you!

GOD WILL PROVIDE

"And my God shall *supply* all your *need*

According to His *riches* in *glory by Jesus Christ.*

Now to our God and Father be glory forever and ever."

Philippians 4:19 (NKJV)

*supply: make (something needed or wanted) available to someone; provide

*needs: is of necessity; necessarily

*need: want; occasion for something; a state that requires relief

*riches: material wealth

*glory: high renown or honor won by notable achievements; take pride or pleasure in

*by: indicating the means of achieving something

*Jesus Christ: the Jewish religious teacher whose life, death, and resurrection as reported by the Evangelists are the basis of the Christian message of salvation

---

My thoughts for today…

In the past, I have always repeated this verse the way I had heard it, as in, "God shall supply all your needs." However, in reading this verse straight from the Bible, it struck me that the Bible is actually saying "need," not "needs."

Therefore, I searched for the different meaning of "need" as opposed to "needs" and became excited by my findings.

The difference between the two words leaves us with no doubt that God not only wants to supply all the things we need, but also our wants!

That being said, the second line of this Bible quote I have also heard differently. I heard it as "according to His riches in heaven." I compared the quote with these words "according to His riches in glory by Jesus Christ."

Ultimately: God supplies all of our needs (and wants) through the achievement (sacrifice) made by Jesus! Amen.

BROKEN SPIRIT

"A merry heart does good, like medicine, but a *broken* spirit dries the bones.

Proverbs 17:22 (NKJV)

* broken: having given up all hope; despairing

My thoughts for today...

Have you ever been broken? For the hurt from a heart that has been broken goes into the very soul. Following the brokenness comes despair and loss of hope, with our dead dreams leaving us bereft, and all passion for life goes out the window.

However, Jesus is the Great Counselor, so while it is fine to share with friends, it is imperative to take it to Jesus. When you unload your pain on Him, it's not simply a Band-Aid as with your friends. For as you share your heart with Jesus, you gradually feel your hope returning. You are given comfort in knowing that He is our one true Help and He has the power to take what was broken and make it whole. Furthermore, Jesus is willing and more than able. I believe that Jesus feels empathy and actually bears our pain as He comes close, absorbing our pain and exchanging it for His peace.

This is my testimony, and I hope this comes to mind when it is your turn to be broken. For truly, to be broken is a part of everyone's spiritual journey.

DON'T LOSE HEART

"I would have lost heart, unless I had believed that I would see the goodness of the Lord in the *land of the living*. Wait on the Lord; be of good courage, and He shall strengthen your heart; Wait, I say, on the Lord!"

Psalm 27:13-14 (NKJV)

*land of the living: not dead; alive

My thoughts for today...

To see clearly, we will need to remove all of our preconceived ideas.

When things are not going our way is the very moment when your faith will be tested the most.

Without hopes and dreams only a bleak future looms ahead.

Life is our training wheels for learning to answer God with "Yes" and "Amen."

Hope encourages us to believe that there are good things just up ahead in our future, that have been ordered by the Lord.

Thank You, God, for my many blessings;

for my eyes that I can see them, my ears that I can hear them,

and for making my heart grateful enough to recognize them!

SPIRITUAL GIFTS

"But one and the same Spirit works all these things, distributing to each one individually as He wills."

1 Corinthians 12:11 (NKJV)

My thoughts for today...

When God imparts to someone a unique spiritual gifting, they will be ridiculed by some and misunderstood by many.

At birth, God breathed into every person a different spiritual gift which is meant to be shared with mankind.

Have you ever been asked about someone you like, concerning the color of their skin, and did you hesitate before answering? This is because you are seeing the person with the eyes of your heart and our hearts don't see color!

Prejudice is a seed and once it gets inside us, this seed of hate spreads and consumes our bodies like a cancer, killing all the good cells of love.

To be or not to be is the question. while just to be is God's answer.

I looked to God and He pointed to Jesus!

BLESSED WHEN WE TRUST GOD

"Blessed is the man who trusts in the Lord

And whose hope is the Lord

For he shall be like a tree planted by the waters

Which spreads out its roots by the river

And will not fear when heat comes

But its leaf will be green.

And will not be anxious n the year of the drought

Nor will cease from yielding fruit."

Jeremiah 17:7-8 (NKJV)

My thoughts for today...

God blesses those who place their trust in Him.

Where does our hope come from?

Our hope comes from the Lord!

Keep your eyes on Jesus,

And feel your fears begin to fade away.

God is more powerful than we can imagine,

More merciful than we can hope for,

And His love is more than enough!

NO CLOCKS IN HEAVEN

"Who lives forever: for His dominion is an everlasting dominion, and His kingdom is from generation to generation."

Daniel 34:5 (NKJV)

My thoughts for today…

"The end of time" means exactly that! For when the world has come to an end and we are in our new heavenly home, there will be no such thing as time because eternity is timeless!

No alarm clocks and no more rushing to meet appointments—sounds heavenly, doesn't it?

Our faith is the core of our being, for we are by God's design.

Give it to God and stay in rest, as He accomplishes those things that are out of your control.

Youth is fleeting, so enjoy it while you still have it!

GOSSIP

"A perverse man sows strife, and a whisperer separates the best of friends."

Proverbs 16:28 (NKJV)

My thoughts for today…

We like to chatter and share all the current news with friends, and we are all guilty of this vice. We greatly enjoy expressing our opinions and most of the time we do not plan to cause harm. But beware, for it is not only others who hear our words of contention, but God hears also.

He listens to His children talking, and we can be sure that our empty chatter displeases our Heavenly Father.

The key to refrain from gossiping as we share news concerning another, is simply to change the subject.

As we add weight around our middles, we inadvertently include a chip on our shoulders.

We ask God for a little healing, just enough to heal the pain.

However, God wants us to ask for total healing, which is to our gain.

NOTHING TOO HARD FOR GOD

'Behold, I am the Lord, the God of all flesh.

Is there anything too hard for Me?"

Jeremiah 32:27 (NKJV)

My thoughts for today...

Be thankful for all things, whether easy or hard, for it is all a part of God's plan and it serves Hs purpose.

Each time God brings a dream to pass it refreshes the soul.

We are all God's creation, designed for His companionship and loved by Him beyond measure.

If you are still alive, God is not finished with you yet!

IF TWO AGREE

"Again, I say to you, that if two of you agree on earth *concerning* anything that they ask, it will be done for them by My Father in heaven. For where two or more are gathered together in My name, I am there in the *midst* of them."

Matthew 18:19-20 (NKJV)

*concerning: on the subject of or in connection with; about

*midst: the middle point or part

My thoughts for today...

While there is power in praying, the more people that are included in the prayer chain, the stronger that prayer becomes! Amen.

Do not worry, for what has been given to you by God cannot be taken away.

The wisest thing that a person can ever do

is to release their will to God's higher will.

VALUE OF A FRIEND

"Two are better than one because they have a good reward for their labor;

For if they fall, one will lift up his companion."

Ecclesiastes 4:9 (NKJV)

"Though one may be overpowered by another, two can withstand him, and a threefold cord is not quicky broken."

Ecclesiastes 9:12 (NKJV)

My thoughts for today…

A strong marriage can be had when a couple includes God,

For this particular strand of three is not easily broken.

When you accept Jesus into your heart, He is with you always, for His is a "forever" kind of love.

No matter how big I dream,

God's dreams are always bigger!

ALL THINGS MADE NEW

"Now I saw a new heaven and a new earth, for the first heaven and earth had passed away. Also, there was not more sea. Then, I, John, saw the holy city, New Jerusalem, coming down out of heaven from God, prepared as a bride adorned for her husband.

And I heard a loud voice from heaven saying, 'Behold, the tabernacle of God is with men, and *He will dwell with them*, and they shall be His people.

God Himself will be with them and be their God.'"

Revelation 21:1-3 (NKJV)

My thoughts for today…

I, personally, consider the above verses to be the most beautiful in the entire Bible, for it is telling us that God Himself will walk among us. This touches my heart every time I read it!

When hearing from God, all things become new, and

the things that used to matter no longer do.

When this world is no more, God will provide us a new world to live in,

And we will drink at the water's edge, which contains living water.

OUR FATHER

"Jesus said to her, 'Do not cling to Me, for I am not yet ascended to My Father:

But go to My brethren and say to them, "I am ascending to My Father and your Father, and to My God and your God."'

John 20:17(NKJV)

My thoughts for today…

Jesus spells it out for us: His Father is <u>our</u> Father, and His God is <u>our</u> God!

Dream bigger dreams and you will fly higher than you can imagine.

The best place to begin your spiritual journey is with "The Lord's Prayer,"

For Jesus began it with, "our Father."

Jesus smiles down at us, wondering at our disbelief!

IN GOD WE TRUST

"To You, O Lord. I lift up my soul.

O my God, I trust in You.

Let me not be ashamed;

Let those be ashamed, who deal treacherously without cause."

Psalm 2 5:1-3 (NKJV)

My thoughts for today…

God never gives up on us and He will never stop loving us.

As a small child looks around, straining to catch a glimpse of his mother, this is how much we need Jesus.

The yearning of man to be close to God is embedded into our hearts from the very beginning, and I believe the closest we ever get to this is when we can look back over our lives, with all their joys and misfortunes, lifting up our hands in praise and thanking God for all of this life's experiences.

Forgive yourself—God already has!

JESUS ASCENDS TO HEAVEN

"Now when He had spoken these things, while they watched,

He was taken up, and a cloud received Him out of their sight."

Acts 1:9 (NKJV)

"And it shall come to pass that whoever calls on the name of the Lord, shall be saved."

Acts 2:21 (NKJV)

My thoughts for today…

To receive a calling from God is to be a prisoner of Jesus Christ.

Where the prison walls are constructed in love

And its bars hold only mercy!

SAVING THE WORLD

"For God sent not His Son into the world to condemn the world; but that the world through Him might be saved."

John 3:17 (NKJV)

My thoughts for today…

As Popeye the Sailor Man famously said, "Well, blow me down!"

This was his way of expressing surprise.

And this is how we feel also, when we realize that to find salvation is not complicated.

And it was never meant to be!

We just need to stop looking at all the reasons we are not ready to be a follower of Jesus Christ, thereby taking the focus off of us and putting it on Him.

So, please consider saying—"Well, blow me down! I want to accept Jesus Christ into my heart."

That's all there is to it.

That was too easy, right?!!

And that's the way God intended it!

God made it easy, because He does not want even one of us to be left behind!

DO NOT THROW STONES

"So when they continued asking Him, He raised Himself up and said to them, 'He who is without sin among you, let him throw a stone at her first.'"

John 8:7 (NKJV)

My thoughts for today…

As children, we have all heard the rhyme, 'Sticks and stones will break my bones, but names will never hurt me." However, you can be assured this is a big thing to God! For simply stated, this is the very opposite of showing love to your neighbor.

And since none of us are perfect, and we all have our faults, it would be wise to keep this in mind when we are tempted to judge or throw stones at another.

For, if Jesus, who is perfect, does not condemn, why should we?

THE SON OF GOD

"Jesus heard that they had cast him out, and when He had found him, He said to him, 'Do you believe in the Son of God?'

He answered and said, 'Who is He, Lord, that I may believe in Him?'

And Jesus said to him, 'You have both seen Him and it is He who is talking with you.'

Then he said, 'Lord, I believe!' And he worshiped Him."

John 9:35-38 (NKJV)

My thoughts for today...

It matters not how you have lived your life.

Only the end results matter.

The here and now.

For when receiving Jesus Christ into your heart,

He will stamp your life

"PAID IN FULL!"

BE PREPARED

"Finally, my brethren, be strong in the Lord and in the power of His might. Put on the whole armor of God, that you may be able to stand against the wiles of the devil.

For we do not wrestle against flesh and blood, but against principalities, against powers, against the rulers of the darkness of this age, against spiritual hosts of wickedness in the heavenly places.

Therefore take up the whole armor of God, that you may be able to withstand in the evil day, and having done all, to stand."

Ephesians 6:10-13 (NKJV)

My thoughts for today…

"BE PREPARED." The Boy Scouts of America use this phrase as their motto.

*Be prepared: to remain in a state of preparedness for any unexpected or uncertain occasion that may arise.

Have you ever wondered how, when life knocks you down, to stay in the fight? I believe it is to be prepared for the unexpected beforehand.

For if you wait until you have been blindsided, you will have no defenses.

So, the key to keeping your peace in the middle of whatever is going on is to pick a few verses that speak to you.

By this, I am referring to the ones that you feel comfortable with. And since this is a very personal thing, you alone can choose them. You can start out with maybe one verse from the Bible, and you can always add more as you go along and have a need.

However, I will share one of my favorites. "He will cover you with His feathers and under His wings you will find refuge." Psalm 91:4

CLOAK OF RIGHTEOUSNESS

"I will greatly rejoice in the Lord.

My soul shall be joyful in my God;

For He has clothed me with the garments of salvation,

He has covered me with the robe of righteousness,

As a bridegroom decks himself with ornaments,

And as a bride adorns herself with her jewels."

Isaiah 61:10 (NKJV)

*cloak: a loose outer garment, as a cape or coat

My thoughts for today....

I believe that the Lord wants us to be clothed in righteousness by faith in Christ's atoning sacrifice on the cross at Calvery.

I'm not qualified to tell you what to do,

Or how to live your life.

I am simply asking you to try on a new coat.

But instead of it being a White House/Black Market kind of brand label, this brand name is Jesus Christ.

And I am only suggesting that you try it on and see if it is a good fit for you.

For I believe, once you do, you will be able to see for yourself just how wonderful it is to feel His warmth and protection, as it radiates in what is a very cold and dangerous world that we live in today.

GOOD AND EVIL

"But of the tree of knowledge of good and evil you shall not eat, for in the day that you that you eat of it you shall surely die."

Genesis 2:17 (NKJV)

My thoughts for today...

I believe that all of the chaos in the world is a "Jack in the Box" effect.

For when Adam and Eve ate of the forbidden fruit, in essence they turned the handle on the box that contained the knowledge of good and evil.

Then the evil was no longer contained, but jumped out of the box upon the earth.

Have you ever played with a Jack in the Box?

Turning the handle and letting Jack pop out of the box is easy but trying to push his head back in to close the lid takes a bit of doing.

Same here.

For, once Jack (evil) was let out, they were unable to

push it back down and so, it still runs rampant upon the earth until this day.

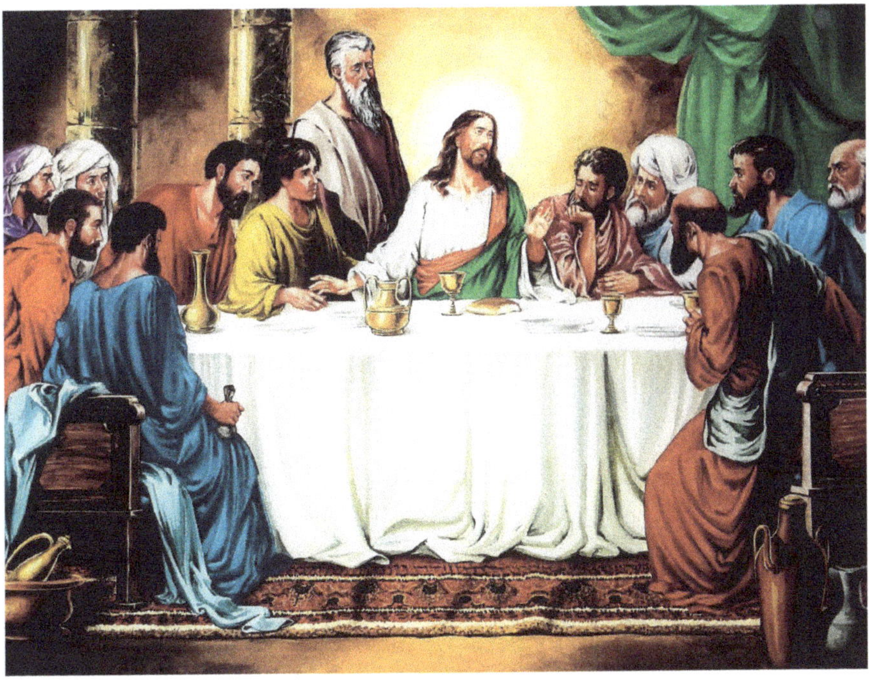

REMEMBER ME

"For I received from the Lord that which I also delivered to you:

That the Lord Jesus on the same night in which He was betrayed took bread:

And when He had given thanks,

He broke it and said,

'Take, eat; this is My body which is broken for you;

Do this in remembrance of Me.'

In the same manner He also took the cup after supper, saying,

This do as often as you drink it,

In remembrance of Me.'"

1 Corinthians 11:23-26 (NKJV)

My thoughts for today...

Each time we take Communion, we are in effect, remembering Jesus,

How He willingly died for us;

and the pain He endured before

ultimately, being nailed to the Cross.

For by His stripes, we are *healed* and by His blood, we are *forgiven*.

*healed: become sound or healthy again; achieving or acquiring wholeness as a person

*forgiven: the act of forgiving; pardon

OUR TIMES ARE IN GOD'S HANDS

"And He said to them, 'It is not for you to know times or season which the Father has put in His own authority.'"

Acts 1:7 (NKJV)

"And you will hear of wars and rumors of wars; see that you are not troubled, for all these things must come to pass. But the end is not yet.

For nation will rise against nation, and kingdom against kingdom

And there will be famines, pestilences, and earthquakes in various places.

All these are the beginning of sorrows."

Mattthew 24:6-8 (NKJV)

My thoughts for today...

As a child, did you ever play the game "Red light, green light?"

Because Jesus is coming back.

And it will be sudden.

Like that childhood game.

"Red light green light….

Here I come!"

And, my beloved brothers and sisters, to get ready

is simply accepting Jesus Christ into our hearts,

as our Lord and Savior,

believing that He is the Son of God.

I AM WITH YOU ALWAYS

"Go, therefore, and make disciples of all the nations, baptizing them in the name of the Father and the Son and of the Holy Spirit, teaching them to observe all things that I commanded you; And lo, I am with you always,

Even to the end of the age.'"
Matthew 28:19-20 (NKJV)

My thoughts for today…

You know, like when you are returning a big-ticket item to a store

and you drop the receipt,

And the wind picks it up and blows it away.

You keep chasing it, trying to grab it

At the expense of looking foolish in front of other people in the parking lot.

Because you HAVE to have to have that receipt!

Well, this is how we should chase after Jesus.

For He is the Way- the ONLY way (our ticket) to gain entry into heaven...

and obtain eternal life!

LOVE IS THE MAIN INGREDIENT

"Owe no one anything except to love one another,

For he who loves another has fulfilled the law."

Romans 13:8 (NKJV)

My thoughts for today...

Don't let others make you feel guilty when you fail to meet all their demands, for your only duty is to love them.

Truly, when we try to please everyone the only thing that we succeed at is exhausting ourselves.

So, while it is good to be kind and helpful to others, beware of the users!

Embracing Jesus means there is nothing in life that we will ever face alone.

A person with considerable character

Has undoubtedly suffered much.

KEEP MOVING FORWARD

"Do not remember the former things,

Nor consider the things of old.

Behold, I will do a new thing,

Now it shall spring forth;

Shall you not know it?

I will even make a road in the wilderness

And rivers in the desert."

Isaiah 43:18-19 (NKJV)

My thoughts for today…

Love will buoy you—and hold your head up.

Helping you to resurface, after life has pulled you down.

As I keep trying to come up higher,

those things that were trying to keep me grounded

have loosened their hold on me.

And although I'm losing things that I once valued.

This no longer matters--

Because I am now free!

LOSS OF A LOVED ONE

"He will wipe away every tear from their eyes, and death shall be no more,

Neither shall there be mourning, nor crying, nor pain anymore, for the former things have passed away.

Revelation 21:3-4 (NKJV)

My thoughts for today...

The loss of a loved one is the hardest thing that can happen to someone.

It matters not if the loss is due to a death, or even a mate walking away,

For pain is pain.

The poet Alfred, Lord Tennyson, said,
"It is better to have loved and lost
Than never to have loved at all."
For love is love.
And the music you heard while being in love
Will follow you always—

And the tune of it will continue to play
And be a gentle hum in the background of your life.

TRUST IN GOD

"Commit your way to the Lord,

Trust also in Him,

And He shall bring it to pass."

Psalm 36:5 (NKJV)

"Delight yourself also in the Lord,

Truust also in Him.

And He shall bring it to pass."

Psalm 36:4 (NKJV)

"Rest in the Lord, and wait patiently for Him."

Psalm 36:7 (NKJV)

My thoughts for today...

Life is a dance and since Jesus knows the way
We simply need to follow His footsteps,
By placing our hands in His
And letting Him lead.

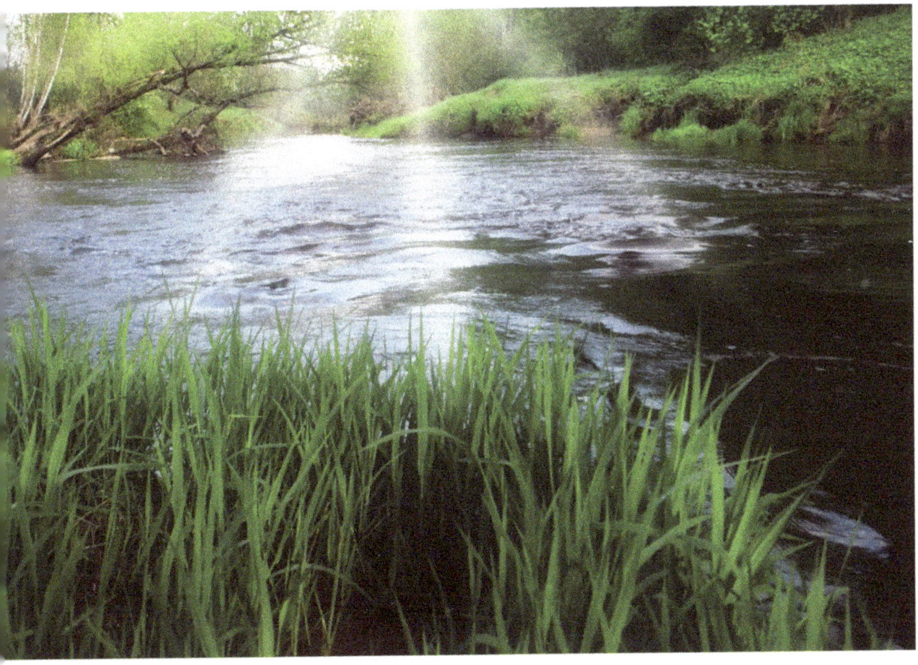

GIFT OF THE HOLY SPIRIT

"Therefore, whoever confesses Me before men,

him I will also confess before My Father in heaven."

Matthew 10:32-33 (NKJV)

"Jesus answered, 'Most assuredly, I say to you, unless one is born of water and the Spirit, he cannot enter the kingdom of God. That which is born of the flesh is flesh, and that which is born of the Spirit is spirit.'"

John 3:5-6 (NKJV)

"Then Peter said to them, 'Repent and let every one of you be baptized in the name of Jesus Christ for the remission of sins and you will receive the Holy Spirit.'"

Acts 2:38 (NKJV)

My thoughts for today…

Many express their opinion that although to be baptized is a good thing,

> it is not really necessary.

However, the reasons to do so are given in the verses above by Jesus, and also by Peter, the disciple whom Jesus described as "on this rock I build My church."

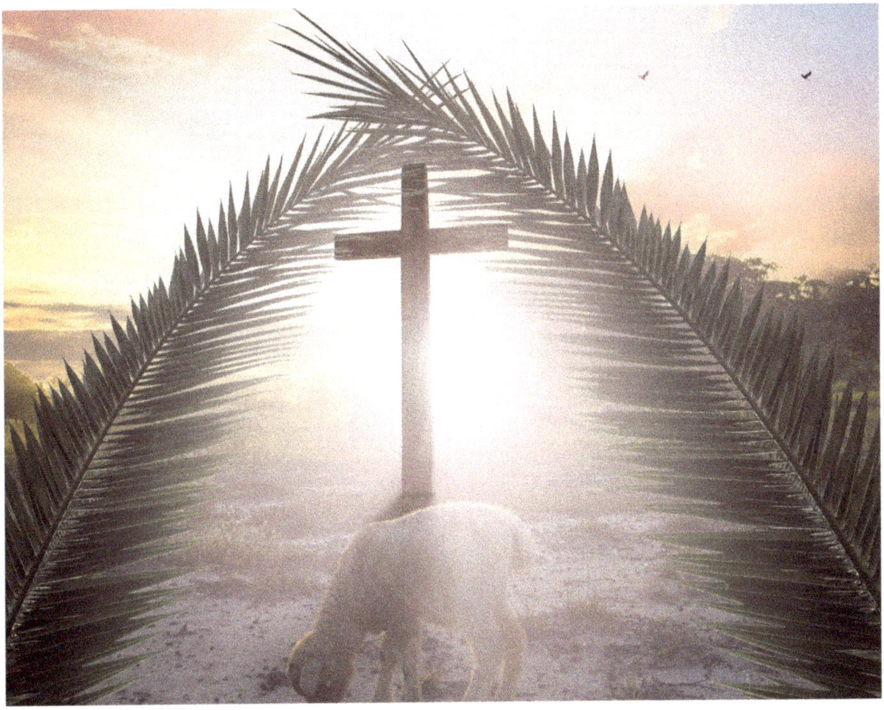

AFTERWORD

To summarize *Take Me to the River* is to emphasize that I believe the Bible is holy, and that the Bible was *inspired* by God, a God who is perfect love.

*inspired: outstanding or brilliant in a way or a degree suggestive of divine inspiration

---

I hold that the Bible is to be treated with the utmost reverence and respect.

The Holy Bible was written by certain prophets and apostles, the latter being hand-picked and chosen by Jesus, and all being led by the Holy Spirit in their writings.

That being said, although God is perfect, the writers of the Holy Bible were not.

They were mostly uneducated people and certainly not perfect, probably less perfect than most, with weaknesses and failings, simply because of the fact that God tends to choose those that others choose to discard.

I truly believe that in doing this, God chooses to show us His power by lifting up the most unlikely, for God chooses the small and the weak to confound the mighty.

So, for those of you who are going through things in your life that are unfair and painful, may I tell you that without a doubt, God sees you!

Now back to the subject of the writers of the Bible. They were human. They had faults and failings, as we all do. They also were raised and taught by parents and the culture of their time. I think we would do well to keep that in mind when reading the Bible, that occasionally these wonderful, imperfect men would insert some of their culture and personal beliefs into their writings. I don't think there is any harm in this, unless this is not taken into account when reading from the Bible.

The bottom line is that God is love. If God's love is not front and center, then we can rest assured that it was not derived from God.

The Holy Bible is our reference point, and I would desire you to set time aside to read it, thereby learning of God's love for the world and of His everlasting love for us. Howbeit, the greatest display of God's immeasurable love being the willing sacrifice of His Son, Jesus Christ, who died to pay the price for our sins.

Shalom

*(Shalom: Hebrew word for peace)

Printed in the USA
CPSIA information can be obtained
at www.ICGtesting.com
CBHW041957021123
1597CB00004BC/9